CW00507461

TABLE OF CONTENTS

INTRODUCTION

I was born in Long Sutton, Lincolnshire, England: a child of the 1950s. To describe the Fenland scenery as dull and the landscape being as flat as a pancake is probably on the generous side.

My mother liked having babies, so maybe my parents were running out of names, because I got called 'Ralph Leslie' after the doctor who delivered me at home - I guess it could have been worse! The 'Cross' bit was my family surname.

I had the kind of childhood that children today can only dream of. I would cycle off with my mates, leaving no clues behind as to where we were going. We climbed trees, jumped over ditches, made dens, played 'cops and robbers' and generally messed about- all innocent stuff of course, except when we nipped into someone's back garden and gorged ourselves on raspberries.

We would return home when hunger pangs were taking over and it usually coincided with mealtime. I was never asked what I'd been doing. At other times, I'd be kicking a football on the back lawn, imitating my idols from Manchester United (a young Bobby Charlton et al), playing with my train set, reading the Beano, or the wonderful 'Famous Five' series, allowing me to escape into a fantasy world.

Everything seemed so stable, reassuring and easy paced. Everyone followed the rules set. No one would dream of cycling on the footpath or not having a bell on their bike. The local policemen would take a dim view of any transgression and yes, they did 'spot checks' on cycle brakes.

I certainly don't take myself seriously and many of the entries are 'tongue in cheek': I'd rather not be seen as a 'fully-fledged, grumpy old man', but actually I don't mind if you do. I have no sense of whether the book will fly off the shelves, or gather dust in a quiet corner, but that's fine by me. Before you say, 'Get a life', I have a very nice one actually, rich and varied, surrounded by family and friends and I am a very tolerant person (my opinion of course).

So, turn the pages and see what makes you go, 'Ah that's exactly how I feel,' and sometimes not!

My thanks go to all those who have suggested 'entries' for the book, especially David Wheeldon and Martin Ewart, who have laughed along with me and at times 'at' me and not forgetting the invaluable contributions from members of my family in helping me put it all together.

Ralph Cross, Wanstead, London

I. TRANSPORT

Cyclists

I am a supporter of cycling and use my own bike now and again, and most cyclists are responsible riders, so I'm certainly not referring to you of course! Cyclists are bound by the same rules as motorists as follows: 'Keep off the pavement and obey traffic signals'.

Pixlr/Joanna Malinowski

'Oh no, it doesn't apply to me,' some obviously believe, as they weave through pedestrians and through the next red traffic light. Maybe they award themselves points for how many times they break the law in a day? It must be a maximum 10 points if they go through a pedestrian crossing with the light on red. As so many cyclists disobey signals, I decided to do my own undercover operation. A doddle to spot one I thought. I spent an hour at traffic signals near where I live, with camera at the ready and NOT ONE cyclist disobeyed the law. All I got was people checking me out as if there was something odd about me just standing there, camera in hand. I put it away and then you know what happened......a cyclist went through on 'red'.

The speed and fury with which some ride, indicates that they are **racing home to beat yesterday's time trial** and nothing will stop them. They are the same people who shout expletives at motorists because a stationary car has not allowed enough space for them to pass by (and go through a red light most likely). They are also the ones who don't use the expensively constructed cycle lanes.

What do those cyclists use their **cameras on their helmets** for- to record their misdemeanours (not just those committed by traffic)? You know they don't.

Bells are compulsory on new bicycles. Please use that bell when you want to pass me on a shared path and if you haven't got one you should get one- very cheap in Poundland- a pound actually. I'd prefer the sound of a bell to the sound of your loud voice, asking me to get out of your way, thank you.

The proliferation of **bike sharing schemes** has had loads of unwelcome spin offs. Some people obviously prefer manual lifting to keep fit, as opposed to cycling, building up their muscles by throwing bikes in canals and rivers. Mobike in Manchester had 10% of its fleet destroyed or stolen. 100 or more of the hire bikes are hauled out of the Thames each year: these were hauled out of the Regent's Canal. One guy declared, 'They keep dumping them on the floor near my house. Next one's going in the skip.'

Electric Bicycles

E-bikes can travel up to speeds of 28mph, yet do not need a licence and therefore technically a 5-year-old (I agree a somewhat oversized one) could ride on one. They have to have a speed limiter, but in some cases, they are removed. As you can imagine, in a cycling country like Holland, the mix of e-bikes and cycles is a real issue because of overtaking amongst the packed cycling lanes. They are testing out technology that automatically cuts the speed of an e-bike right down in built up areas. 65 people died in 2022 in Holland on such bikes. What about

Pexels.com/Kate Trifo

e-bikes needing a registered number plate, with the rider wearing a crash helmet as for a motorcyclist and a minimum age of 16?

The police are reporting that **e-bikes are now used extensively in theft**, particularly of mobile phones. The classic style is the 'two on a bike'; from statistics they are almost exclusively male teenagers. They snatch the phone from the pedestrian and are out of sight in minutes and can escape up alleyways that no police car can follow.

Electric Scooters

What I mean here are the scooters that look like a big version of a child's scooter, not an electric Lambretta or a Vespa! This is what the law says: '*It is only legal to use an e-scooter on private land with the permission of the land owner. Where a trial rental scheme is running, it's legal to use a rental e-scooter on a public road or cycle lane, provided you have the correct licence and follow road traffic regulations.*'

You don't have to wait long to see one on the road, or weaving amongst pedestrians. In the photo, you will notice the scooter on the wrong side of the road. He was no more than 14 years of age. The other law breaker is on Wanstead High Street. As there seems to be no locking system to keep them secure, the owner seems to take them everywhere with them, but I've not seen one wheeled into a cubicle in public toilets…yet.

In their wisdom, Transport for London have banned e-scooters on buses and the tube on the basis that there have been cases of explosions of batteries recorded (although I've spotted a few who've managed it). Paris has banned the use of e-scooters- despite the fact that rental companies had put (invested in) 15,000 of them around the city. We will lag behind for sure until the government eventually (unlikely) realise they are a menace unless controlled with number plates and compulsory helmets: 'Some chance,' I hear you say.

Pedestrians

Zebra crossings with flashing warning lights, or 'Belisha beacons' were introduced in 1934 by the Minister of Transport, Mr Belisha. Over time, many were replaced by Pelican crossings, with lights to stop traffic. Can you think of anything more irritating as a motorist, seeing the lights turn red with no pedestrians, as they walked when they spotted a gap in the traffic (not a problem for some cyclists of course!). Common sense is beginning to prevail, with the return of the zebra crossing, but with the retention of pelican crossings on busy streets, where otherwise traffic would be constantly at a standstill.

I'm sure you know, the title is 'pedestrian' crossing, rather than '*ride my bike across*' crossing. I saw a furious altercation between a motorist and cyclist when the latter just went straight across without warning and the man on the bike was within a whisker of being crushed. Lesson learnt? I think not.

Cars

Now let's start off with something that is becoming increasingly commonplace: what I call '**throaty engines**'. You know what I mean; the engine that has been souped up (apparently with a modified 'air to fuel' ratio), supposedly to impress, as the car roars down the high street for 50 metres until of course it meets another vehicle and has to stop. That, however,

Pexels.com/Eric McLean

is the moment the individual will rev the engine up and then, the 'pièce de resistance', as the vehicle moves off, a sound like gunshots can be heard; 'backfiring' is the term I believe.

I think these people are nicknamed 'boy racers'. The car seat has to lean backwards of course and the driver is likely to have a baseball cap (back to front). These people must have low self-esteem and need to feel noticed. Maybe a bit of psychiatric help could sort that out, or a policeman standing at one end of the high street and another at the other end. A car passes making a racket, the officer radios ahead, the other steps out (be careful!), signalling the driver to stop. The word soon gets around that the law is 'feeling their collar'.

Why is there the desire of some to own the biggest vehicle they can buy that isn't quite an HGV, to drive around the town in? The nickname for an **SUV** - 'Chelsea Tractor' - comes from the fact there are more per head of population in Chelsea and Kensington than anywhere else. Steve Gooding of the RAC said, *'It is right to question if suburban drivers need a car capable of ploughing over rivers, across fields and up steep hills just to pop to the shops,"*

Andrew Simms, from the New Weather Institute (www.newweather.org), said: *'Advertising has somehow persuaded urban families that they need the equivalent of a two-tonne truck to go shopping, and that is a problem.'*

The size of an SUV- its width and length- is creating problems in car parks and on the streets. Why should a driver of say a 'Smart' Car, pay the same to park; after all it is half the length of a typical SUV (2.5m compared to 5m) and 17cm (7") narrower?

Living in London, I no longer own (or need) a car. While on buses, I notice that **drivers will NOT wait and allow the bus to pull out** after picking up passengers. This is despite the fact that they will most likely pass by the bus at the next stop. When I lived in Norwich, I had a car and always let taxis out from side roads in the city, as they need to make a living by getting from fare to fare as reasonably quickly as possible. A taxi driver told me he gets let out more easily in his private car than when in his taxi!

Depositphotos/Zsolt Joo

With so much traffic on the roads, it makes sense to **keep to the speed limits.** Why do some travel way below it frustrating drivers who then, foolishly, try to overtake? Have you ever been travelling at a decent speed in the outer lane of the motorway and come across what can only be described as a greedy driver, or a fool- take your pick, staying in that lane. 'Undertaking' is not allowed, so what do you do? Flashing your lights only increases their resolve to stay put.

'Improvements' on the M25 have meant it is now four lanes, to help with congestion. Unfortunately, many drivers stay one lane from the outside, like on a three-lane motorway and the inside lane is empty, or rather used by speeding motorists, who zig zag at 80mph or more, between the two inside lanes. Congestion is as bad as it ever was.

Satellite Navigation has revolutionised driving, but there's always a down side, because we are losing our sense of logic and direction and without those two things, *BIG* mistakes are possible. The 'get- away' driver for a group of bank robbers had the addresses for 12 banks on his sat nav, which the police found rather useful as evidence. A minicab driver took a passenger, who wanted to see Chelsea play at Stamford Bridge, all the way north to Stamford Bridge in Yorkshire. She missed the game.

Black cab drivers still use their memories to get them around London streets. They train for between two and four years and then can remember 25,000 streets and 20,000 landmarks in London. Research has shown that their brains actually grow during this training period. Wow!

Caravans & Motor Homes

Ah, the joys of travel on an Easter weekend, when the caravans and motorhomes are dusted down for the first time of the year and given an airing on the open road. As they amble along at 40mph, they remain oblivious to all else, focused on the exciting prospect of parking up to share the pleasure of caravanning with like-minded people in rain sodden, muddy fields. Each to their own, but not for me. As a child I did delight in staying in a caravan every summer, except for the sounds, sight and smell of an outdoor portable toilet.

Shutterstock

Lorries

You are cruising along a dual carriageway at 70 mph when a **lorry decides to overtake another,** usually when they are moving uphill. You are  the car behind and your speed drops to 40 mph and the two goods' vehicles 'sit' side by side for the next mile or so, as the difference in speed is minimal. The empty lorry (probably empty) gets to the brow of the hill, overtakes and returns to the left-hand lane. Lo and behold the loaded lorry (it likely is), that has been overtaken, now picks up speed because of its weight and catches up with the empty lorry. Just to add to your frustration, the leading lorry turns off at the next junction, just as you predicted.

Railways

Why is there not a greater drive to get **freight off roads** and on to rail, as our roads become more and more clogged? Companies like Tesco and Stobart are to be congratulated on their efforts to ship logistics by rail.

HS2: what a complete shambles! The argument was that the West Coast Main Line could not cope with the amount of freight and passengers competing for 'pathways'. The cost was estimated at £100 billion, including over 500 bridges or viaducts. HS2 will save just 29 minutes on the journey to London from Birmingham and passengers will end up at Old Oak Common (where?) and not Euston, until modifications are completed at this station, if ever.

Surely, parts of the West Coast Main Line could have been made into four tracks and other diversionary (closed) routes reinstated (such as parts of the old Great Central Route, starting from London). £100 billion buys a lot of railway around the UK, especially where in so many cases, the old track bed is still in place.

Even the complex scheme to rebuild the line from Oxford to Cambridge is priced at just £5 billion, but the last leg is in doubt because of value versus cost. The North, which feels let down by the axing of the complete HS2 scheme, should at least get major improvements with the sort of money that will be available now..

Passenger traffic has dropped so much, with businesses using programs such as Zoom or Teams, to meet their needs in the 'Home office'. According to the latest figures from the Office of Rail and Road, rail passenger journeys (2023) are now at 56.9% of the 1.739 billion journeys made pre-pandemic.

Aeroplanes

I'm settling down in my seat for my five-hour flight. Wow, they actually have **'fold back' seats** (forget most airlines then). All seems well until 'wham', the 'kind' person in front drops his or her seat back- not nice. I am not alone. Most people agree it is not good etiquette to simply recline your seat, affecting the person behind. In October 2022, a survey in the US by 'thevacationer.com' found that 77% of travellers said they thought it rude to fully recline their seat. Of those, more than 27% said they would still lean back, but politely ask if it was ok first. Good

Depositphotos/vsurkov

for them, but that's not my experience.

I enjoy flying, and look forward to a relaxed journey on to my destination. I might even doze for a time. However, **babies and young children** do not like flying and make their annoyance abundantly clear to their parents in the way they know best, but unfortunately, we must all share in the consequent 'volcanic eruption'. I must admit that as parents come on board a flight with a young child, I am praying (yes I am actually praying), that they don't sit in that vacant seat behind, or even opposite, or even five seats back. Don't be fooled by gaps in the screaming: the adorable little one is simply building up strength for the next round. Earplugs are a must. Even some children struggle to cope with the screeching, as the young lady in the picture on the previous page is hinting at!

Vecteezy/agussetiawan99

There is however, one thing I fear most. What if a morbidly obese person comes to sit next to me? How on earth are they going to wedge in that seat without claiming most of my personal space? These days, my expanding frame needs a complete seat for itself.

Surely, if someone is so expansive that they require a seat belt extension, they should be paying for two seats. Scoot budget airlines certainly agree and a spokesperson stated, *'If you are a guest 'of size' who requires two seats, fares and fees for two guests apply.'*

What is a 'guest of size' I ask? Before Ryanair et al get in quick, there will be challenges in the courts if it becomes widespread (sorry for the pun). Air Canada lost a court case for internal flights, when trying to do exactly that (cbc.ca) and in Australia, the 'Obesity Collective' (what?), says such rules cause embarrassment and are discriminatory. (www.theobesitycollective.org.au)

I have seen some passengers dealing stoically with it, though the look on their face indicates the flight could be a trial for them- *and* the physically challenged individual. In January 2023 Arthur Berkowitz boarded a flight from Alaska to Philadelphia. As he went to take his aisle seat, he describes how a 'morbidly obese' passenger took up so much space, he could not fit in. The flight was completely full, so he had to stand the whole way. (CNN.com)

Have you ever brought along your case to put in the plane's hold and found it's fractionally over the 23kg you've paid for and I mean *fractionally*, maybe the weight of a jar of jam? Obviously one option is to open your case and start frantically pulling out anything that might help to reduce the weight.

Of course, this does two things: it annoys those behind you in the queue and you've nowhere else to stuff those things anyway. Your 'carry on' luggage is already bulging and full. Well, there's no option; the airline demands you pay extra for the **overweight bag**. Count yourself lucky if it's EasyJet - it's only £12 per flight. I won't tell you what BA charges.

The thing is, the guy behind you in the queue, weighs 20 stone (127kg) and yet he's not paying a penny more for his ticket, compared to the 10 stone (63kg) lightweight next to him. I have the perfect solution. We should be **weighed before flying** and charged accordingly.

We could have four bands, A (lightest), B, C and D. You buy your ticket at home as usual, knowing your 'rating' according to your trusty bathroom scales. You then casually hop on and off purpose-built scales at the airport - the reading unseen by anyone but those at the check in desk (though their expression might give it away). 99% of people would have correctly identified their category before arrival. Those who didn't would have to pay extra. Mind you they might hold up the queue by rushing off to the toilet to achieve the necessary reduction in weight.

What a wonderful incentive to lose weight prior to your holiday and reduce pressure on the NHS: less people with diabetes type two, or heart attacks. I'd probably be a 'C', so there's no self interest in my suggestion. Just one catch, while away, you'd be forced to eat meagre rations and drink less on your all-inclusive vacation, to avoid an additional charge for your return flight.

Before you consider my idea is completely ridiculous/unworkable (surely not!), some airlines are clearly aware of the issues. Samoan people are the most overweight in the world, so on journeys to Pago Pago, Hawaiian Airlines weigh passengers to ensure the plane is balanced – seats are not pre-allocated, to avoid the plane tipping sideways out of the sky (beatofhawaii.com). Samoa Air and Uzbekistan started weighing passengers in 2015 (smh.co.au). Maybe I'll suggest it to Ryanair.

Why is it that I always choose the wrong queue to line up at the check-in desk or at passport control? I weigh it up and decide *this* line will be much faster. Failed…..again.

Buses

Now let's hear it for those **bus drivers** out there who give you a cheery welcome as you get on the bus. 'When was that?' I hear you say.

I do sometimes feel drivers regard it as a nuisance to have passengers on their bus. I'm always on the lookout for 'positive' drivers and I have 'reported' them to their operators for being just normal, friendly and cheerful. My experience indicates that female drivers engage with passengers far more (and are better drivers!).

I was speaking to a young driver, praising him for his cheery manner as people got on and off a bus. He simply said, *'I love my job and it makes me happier if I am positive and you get a lovely response back from people. Some drivers hate their work and just do it as they have to earn a living.'*

As a retiree/senior citizen, I have my **'freedom pass'** - my ticket to trave*l on* public transport at no cost. I overheard a gent say to his friend, *'Tomorrow I'm going to get on any bus and see where it takes me; have a stroll and a cup of tea somewhere and then just come back home. Perfect.'*

While no derogatory comment could counteract the joy of my 'Freedom Pass', I was a little disappointed to hear a bus driver in Norwich refer to it, on a call to his depot, as the, 'Old Biddy Pass', clearly a name in common usage amongst 'First' bus drivers in that city.

Shutterstock/Boibin

II. JARGON

I am baffled and amused in equal measure by the **phrases and terminology** that have crept into our language in the last few years. It is ironic that in an age when we do all we can to make things more straightforward, be it through voice activation, or remote control, we will say something in ten words when three would do.

The old (right?) way	The New Version
Now	At this moment in time
In future	Looking forward
I	I myself personally
These	These ones
Worst possibility	Least-worst option
In the end	At the end of the day
Now	In the here and now

Americanisms

As indicated above, they are everywhere, so here's just a few more to throw in. In the past, when the electric supply went off, maybe in a thunderstorm, we called it a power cut or power failure. Now it's called a 'power outage'? What kind of name is that? If convicted of an offence, you no longer 'appeal *against* the verdict', oh, no you 'appeal the verdict'.

Why do people now say leverage as 'levverage' When it should be pronounced as 'leeverage)? It is harassment (say it quickly), not 'ha-rass-ment'. Even on the hallowed BBC, you'll hear either of those (is that 'eether' or 'either'?!)

There's also, what was once a trend, but is now commonplace in the UK and really embedded in Australia as well as the USA, which is known as 'up talking', or the use of **'high rise terminals'**.

This is when the speaker raises his or her voice at the end of a sentence so as to sound as if they are asking a question. If you don't know what I mean, simply go to YouTube and put in 'High rise terminals', or 'Up talking'.

I've noticed in the UK, that when a major incident happens and people are hurt or badly injured, our politicians rush to show empathy to the victims. They say, somewhat inanely, that their thoughts and prayers are with those concerned. A) do they actually pray? B) how many milliseconds before their thoughts move on to their next 'project'?

Daft

Our hallowed BBC has some things to answer for. 'When 'handing back' to the presenter (actually they don't hand back anything), the reporter will say the presenter's name as if he or she doesn't

Vecteezy/Wawan Setiawan

know the item is done with. One of the weather forecasters always needs to tell us '*That's your weather.*' I know it was the weather. It wasn't 'Gardeners' Question Time' was it?

Why do we say, 'Least-worst option or 24/7?' What do we mean by, 'People stop at nothing'? Don't they ever stop for something? What about, 'I saw it with my own eyes.' Not with anyone else's then I presume.

Mispronunciations

When I was teaching younger children, I found it interesting, indeed amusing, that they mispronounced or said two words in particular incorrectly. One was computer = pooter, and skeleton = skellington. I remember listening to the children singing along to "I am the Lord of the Dance (said He)' and felt sure it wasn't quite right. I discovered that they thought it was: 'I am the Lord of the Dance *settee.'*

Adults give it a good go too, though maybe I should just put it down to linguistic change rather than linguistic decay. The most common errors seem to be:

- Expresso (espresso),
- Pacific (specific),
- Prostrate cancer (prostate cancer),
- Artic (Arctic),
- Renumeration (remuneration).

Do you know which way round is correct? Of course you do!

Dialect

We are blessed with so many different dialects from all over the country, so as a breather from making you cross, maybe I can make you smile. I was brought up in South Lincolnshire and as a result I say things in a certain way that some people find amusing. Get a life I say. They claim that I say 'carpet', 'party', 'human' in a ridiculous way. What's wrong with 'caaarpit', 'paaarty' and 'hoomun'? Moreover, I apparently say days of the week incorrectly. I will write them as they should be said correctly (of course): Satdi, Sundi, Mundi, Tuesdi, etc. I am supported in that by the people of 'Notinham', 'Lesta', and 'Daarby' who have a similar intonation.

Norfolk is a great place to live (I was there for around 35 years) and you'll hear some interesting 'twists' I can tell you. '*I hent been to Narridge for a long toime*' = 'I haven't been to Norwich for a long time.' If you like going out running for exercise, I guess you'd call that 'jogging'. Wrong, in Norfolk it's pronounced *'jargon'*.

A child in school came up to me and said, *'My dad's got another 'boot' so now he's got two boots.'* I thought, well how long has his poor parent been hopping around on one? You know better of course; his dad now had two boats to use on the '*Narfak Broads*'.

The North East beats us hands down of course with the use of words like canny, pet and aye, plus delightful phrases such as '*geet walla*' (very large) or, '*That gadgie's gannin' proper radgie like.*' That translates as 'That man is extremely cross.' I love it all!

The Death of the Apostrophe

Sad to say, it's on its way out (notice the correct usage there), albeit not just yet and only when the computer says 'yes'.

Let's be honest here, we can understand the word 'wasn't', with or without an apostrophe, as with 'haven't' and 'couldn't', although we say 'don't' in a way that would technically change if it was written as 'dont'.

The 'Apostrophe Protection Society' (yes it does exist), crusades for the retention of the apostrophe and its correct usage. For me the ending of the apostrophe would have one benefit- we'd stop seeing the signs such as potato's or tomato's on the greengrocer's market stall.

Attempts to Impress

Now I have been accused of using the odd **more complex word** as I talk, but in fairness, I had it drilled into me by my teachers that using the word 'said' continually in my writing was not big and was not clever. I therefore diversified, trying to make my writing scintillating, striking, graphic etc. However there comes a point when it gets a bit silly.

On becoming a Schools' Adviser, I realised I was working with some individuals who clearly studied their thesaurus. Suddenly the word 'general' was a 'no no'. It had to be *'generic'*. Education was out, *'pedagogy'* was in.

It was some of those same (decent actually) people who, on my return from the **Tate Modern** in London, could not understand why I mocked an exhibit entitled 'An Oak Tree'. It was actually a glass of tap water on a shelf. Apparently, my mind was 'too closed'. I regarded that as a compliment. I intend to revisit at some point. This time I will turn up with, hidden under my jacket, a glass containing a pale-yellow liquid. When it is safe to do so, I will place my own display next to the 'Oak Tree' with a piece of folded card stating that my exhibit is, 'Taking the Piss'.

One of my favourite periodicals is '**Railway Magazine**' (and why not?). Even they have 'lost it'. They refer to 'ingress' (water in a steam locomotive's boiler), 'extant' (still in existence), the 'consist' (a train), 'ubiquitous' (the type of railway locomotive found everywhere), myopic (short sighted i.e. not thought through) and 'miasma' (the smell or vapour left in the air by a steam locomotive).

III. BUILDINGS

Plastic

Now plastic UPVC windows are a practical solution in many cases. They are integrated within modern buildings reasonably successfully, without looking unpleasant; most building contractors go for a decent design.

My major gripe is with the householders and councils, who prioritise cheap over looks, when they replace, say, a beautiful wooden sash (sliding) window in a Victorian property. UPVC sash windows look OK, but are more expensive, so they go for a less expensive window that opens outwards. Most of us like to see shapes that are symmetrical, but another way to cut costs is to have maybe one window opening, which just looks plain ugly.

Preserving Our Heritage

We should be careful what we wish for. It is easy to sweep aside the past, assuming that new is better. Few of us applaud the buildings that replaced those suffering war damage, put up thoughtlessly in the 1950s and 60s. Yet, for economy, or whatever, the original charm of the left side of this elegant building has been destroyed.

Solar Panels

Unless put discreetly into a new building, where they are slotted into a recess and matched to the tile colour, they can look absolutely awful. I'd rather have a  wind farm in sight than roof panels any day.

IV. POLITICS

Sadly, the **decline in standards** in politics and the fractures in society, came about chiefly due to the influence of the Brexit referendum, where friends and families sat on opposite sides of

Pexels/Dylan Bueltel

the divide and the press and social media stirred and undermined the tolerance people showed towards each other.

Throughout the debate, insults and inaccuracies were bandied about. An unfounded statement was made that Turkey would soon be joining the EU. The rolling out of a bus, emblazoned with the promise that we could save £350 million a week for the NHS if we left, was a dishonest claim. It did not take into account a plethora of benefits, including the many improvements made in the UK with EU funding.

Of course, propaganda was bandied about on both sides and George Osbourn the Chancellor warned that there would be education and defence cuts and tax hikes if we left.

The evidence shows if we had put the vote in the hands of those under 50, we would have remained in the EU. I said at the time, anyone over 60 should have been **disenfranchised** for that issue- you think I'm joking, but I'm not. You can change the government every five years but not Brexit.

Of course, the saying, **'never trust a politician'** is perhaps a good starting point. For too many, loyalty starts and finishes with having an eye on the big prize. The Labour Party had a man who voted 428 times against his party's line when a backbencher, but then expected loyalty from others when he became leader of the opposition - Jeremy Corbyn - do you remember him?

The slipperiest eel, with no thought to anyone but himself, is a certain Boris Johnson (Leader of the Boris Party). How come it took so long for people to get the fact that **clowns belong in the circus**? You must have heard the saying, *'All mouth but no trousers'*? That suits him rather well don't you think? Here's a man with at least 8 children, who in 2007, in an article in the Telegraph stated that, *'The primary challenge facing our species is the reproduction of the species itself.'* Hypocrite comes to mind.

Twisting the truth comes natural to him, like many politicians. Do you remember his constant diatribe about more nurses and doctors - even though it takes years to train them, so we pinch them from 'developing' countries, putting their health systems close to collapse?

The most 'dodgy' claim he made was about 40 **new hospitals**. Many of those were extensions anyway and the boss of one NHS trust said, "'There's a 0% chance there's going to be that number of new hospitals by 2030. We'll be moderately lucky to have eight.

The solution to the 'boo hah' politics is simple: **proportional representation** (PR). The current system has kept Labour and Conservatives in power. How can it be fair that in 2019, the Conservative Party won 43.6% of the popular vote, yet had an 80-seat majority? The Liberal Democrats won 11 seats, yet had 11.5% of the vote, which with PR would have been 74. PR would therefore allow new or existing minority parties the opportunity to grow as the people chose. Internationally, under 100 countries around the world choose 'first past the post' and the majority are former UK colonies, like Bermuda, Uganda and Jamaica.

V. HYGIENE

Now let's get this straight, I am not the tidiest, cleanest person you could come across, but I could be worse. After all, I shower every day, wear clean clothes, wash my hands regularly and usually wash my fruit before eating.

Toilets

It's a strange thing but I don't mind sharing a toilet seat used by family and friends, but even a clean public toilet (not many of those), requires me to wipe around the seat with paper several times.

Did you know that a lot of men do not wash their hands after holding their 'member' in the toilet? Ok I haven't stood watching, making a tally, but my estimate is that 20% come out without cleaning hands; some even after they've been 'busy' in a cubicle! Maybe that's why I either open the door to the gents' toilets with my little finger or knuckle, alternatively hoping that someone comes in and I can dash out of the door without touching it at all.

There is a new phenomenon: men who have the ability to wee at the same time as scrolling their phone in their other hand. None of that bears thinking about. That's why I will not eat shared crisps or snacks in a public place as they may contain all kinds of unpleasant bacteria from people you have never met and wouldn't want to after that.

Have you ever held a hosepipe ready to water something in the garden? You are pointing at the plant, ready to go. You switch on the water: I defy you to aim accurately. Well, transfer that to a male desperate to 'go'. Get the picture? Transfer that to the increasing tendency to have gender neutral toilets and you'll have an unpleasant environment for ladies- even worse as some men don't even bother to lift the seat.

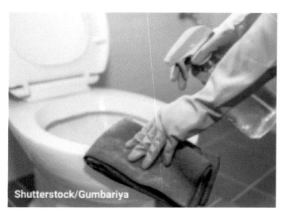
Shutterstock/Gumbariya

One thing I notice is that many people do not put the lid down on a toilet when flushing it. Harpic did some research using high speed camera technology and it showed that with the lid up, thousands of tiny aerosol droplets, containing bacteria and viruses can reach a surface two metres away.. Yet it is estimated that 55% of adults don't close the lid.

Bathroom manufacturer Ponte Giulio commissioned research into the cleanliness of public toilets. Here are the areas containing bacteria, from the *least to the most:*: soap dispenser, mirror, toilet flush handle, hand dryer, under the toilet, toilet seat, waste bin, side wall, floor, toilet paper dispenser, hand rail, tap, radiator, sink. Those last three contained much more bacteria than the rest put together. Maybe I *don't* need to wipe that toilet seat when I'm in the public toilet.

More Bacteria!

OK, so you may have thought we'd covered this already, but this is a slightly different slant. The washroom nightmare is when the soap dispenser is empty, or there's a sticky, shared bar of white soap- well it was white when it was first put out.

Hot air hand dryers are considered to be the hygienic way to dry your hands. Apparently the 'jet'/turbo type you see around increasingly, can propel viruses up to three metres if the person's hands haven't been washed sufficiently with soap. Paper towels for me then.

Don't borrow someone's mobile phone. A survey in Northern Ireland indicated that 15% of mobile, or desk phones had enough bacteria to cause infections. Use the phone by all means, but have the sanitiser close by. Petrol pump handles are not exempt either. They estimate that one handle is used by around 200 people a week. Research in the USA by 'GripHero' gloves indicated that pump handles can be 1,100 times more contaminated than a toilet seat, so make sure you use the gloves provided on the forecourt-much nicer than holding someone else's nozzle!

Picking noses is more prevalent than you think. According to those prepared to admit it, 95% of Americans asked the question, confessed to picking their noses occasionally and 45% said they did it in public. 23% said they jabbed their fingers up between five and ten minutes at a time. I'm sure it can't be like that in the UK! Other things to watch out for when it comes to bacteria- the restaurant menu and the condiments.

Sneezing

Smaller cough and sneeze droplets can travel up to 60 metres. They interact with the gas cloud emitted, hence the distance they can travel.

We may be caught out without a tissue to cover our nose and mouth, but a shirt sleeve has got to be better than doing nothing, which would otherwise spread germs across the cake stall.

Swimming Pools & Outdoor Hot Tubs

I accept that swimming is an activity that gives so much pleasure to so many people and makes a big contribution to keeping people healthy and fit. It is an essential skill for children to learn from an early age, as one day it might just save their life.

Pexels/Sinasi Muldur

Unfortunately for me it all started badly, I presume as a child, as I have a fear of the water and although I can actually swim, the depth of the water must not go above my neck. I get all tense and breathe heavily. I can't bear the thought of having a heart attack while doing the thing I dislike so much!

My desire not to enter a pool in an indoor setting, is exacerbated by the steamy atmosphere and 'yucky' smell of chlorine getting up my nose and in my eyes. Add to that the hair lying around on the changing room floor and the sight of a discarded plaster.

Outdoor hot tubs in people's back gardens were once all the rage: I never understood this silly idea. The peculiar pastime of sitting in the bubbling water, glass of prosecco in hand with neighbours you hardly knew, looking up at the night sky, appeared to be over, tubs seen as unfashionable and outdated. Now apparently there's a bit of a resurgence. Before you order one, be aware that they must be maintained and cleaned regularly. Dr Freestone from the University of Leicester recommends people shower before and after their dip. I don't need to explain why.

Pexels.com/Sinasi Muldur

VI. FOOD & DRINK

Knives and Forks

I was brought up to eat my food, holding my fork in the left hand and my knife in my right- a rule applying to all, whether right or left-handed. That was the standard way

Pexels/Karolina Grabowska

universally taught in my day. My wife and I brought our children up to use cutlery correctly and they still manage very successfully. What has happened to this most civilised of practices?

EatRio.net

I can understand why we pick up pizza with our hands and let's be honest, fish and chips somehow taste better eaten directly from the packaging with our fingers. Again, it's the American influence: cut or pull with a knife in the left hand and jab

SKIN&INK

OTHING

NYC | AKR

INANDINK.COM

down with the fork to pick up, pointing variously between 45 and 90 degrees. I've also noticed that the knife and fork seem to have become an extension of the hand, so you will see people gesticulating with their cutlery pointing at the ceiling.

Drinking

If I'm in a bar and order a drink, and it's in a bottle, the cap is taken off and I'm handed it, as it is. Are they trying to save on glasses or something? I actually have to ask

depositphotos/Andrew Loovya

for a glass to pour it in! It tastes much nicer out of a glass (as does coffee in a crockery cup). I look around and everyone under 50 seems to like drinking out of that narrow little bottle spout: why?

Food Packaging

What is fun about those bags of mini chocolate bars called **'Fun Size'**? You end up eating three bars to make it fun.

Why do cucumbers come in a plastic wrap? They say it's to provide a barrier to germs and 'contaminants', since cucumbers are mostly eaten with the skin on. Why aren't grapes individually wrapped then? Individual apples don't come wrapped up, nor do pears or tomatoes quite often.

Pasta bags come with a sticky strip, apparently to reseal the bag for the next usage.

Irritatingly they just don't work - in fact they are completely useless. You stick the top down and it flips up every time.

'Best Before' Dates

Common sense prevails at last! I would also argue that the 'use by date' can be exceeded (especially dry products), if the food looks OK and smells fine. That's what happened when I was a child and indeed growing up, and look, I'm still here to tell the tale. More people get stomach upsets from food that is undercooked.

In the Restaurant

When you are actually in a restaurant and are choosing from a menu, how often does the waiter respond to your request, say for a glass of tap water with the phrase 'no problem'? Well it had better not be. There are even occasions when you choose an item and they say, 'Good choice'. Maybe I should ask for jelly and custard on top of my roast beef and see if I get the same response.

I do like buffets, where you choose what you want. It's the only time you can put chow mein, pizza, Yorkshire pudding and gravy, mixed up on the same plate. The downside; it is at times a free for all, with people rushing from one 'station' to another as if the food is running out.

In a similar vein, when you go **all-inclusive** on holiday, you will see greedy, wasteful people piling food on their plates, as if it's going out of fashion. You just know they will walk away, leaving a mountain of left-over food to be thrown in the bin. Unfortunately, the 'all you can eat' opportunity a buffet offers, can be a problem for those with eyes bigger than their stomachs and I have noticed that in these settings, there is a disproportionate number of people I would describe as **obese++.**

'Seen but not heard' was the old adage that applied to us as children- not very kind or appropriate when you think about it. I remember that rule- really from my grandparents' era, began to loosen in the fifties. Even then we wouldn't dream of wriggling in our seats or saying we were bored. Now, with the advent of mobile phones and electronic devices, children are 'heard but not seen', as they slide down  into their dining chair below table level, focused totally on the equipment they are holding. Some don't even stop when the food is served: the phone or device is propped up against an object. Presumably eating food is so boring, they need entertainment when eating. I am also, in fact, referring here to eating out in a restaurant! Mind you, you will also notice adults looking at their phones, rather than the person they are with.

Depositphotos/Guys_who_shoot

Eating on Public Transport

Why do people think it is acceptable to bring their KFC or McDonald's take away meal on the bus or tube? You are on your way home after a delicious three-course meal in a restaurant and you are feeling replete. Try not to feel queasy, when your nostrils are filled with the smell of a quarter pounder or a fourteen-piece 'party bucket'. Please eat up before travelling.

I don't know about you, but breakfast for me is quite sufficient with cereal or maybe toast. How dreadfully anti-social and stinky it was to be sat opposite a guy eating a curry and rice at 9 o'clock last Monday morning on the tube. I love Indian food but not then thank you. My tissue came in useful as an alternative to its usual purpose.

VII. A BIT IRRITATING

Queues

Queueing is a very British thing, though Americans will often 'form a line'. Don't expect to be first on a bus while on holiday anywhere abroad, even if you're the first waiting at the stop. However the Japanese, as you can imagine, are very conscious of the need to 'wait in line'. In Israel though, there's a saying that, *'The shy always lose'.* No queueing there then.

Why is it that someone in the queue gives the person in front space that would take five people. We're not talking about an ATM machine or doctor's surgery. It happens in

Shutterstock/ThamKCg

my Tesco Express and I want to make clear this is not a hangover from Covid – it precedes that time. I just want to give them the gentlest of nudges in the back to move them forward.

I'm at the supermarket and I'm unloading my trolley ready to be served by the checkout operator. Of course, I have my loyalty card and credit card at the ready. The person in front is about to

51

pay, so it won't be long before I'm through. Wrong: s/he is having a little conversation with the till operator about how the day has gone so far and then of course it will take the next five minutes to find the right card.

Whistling

Why do old people whistle? When I was a lad, it was common for the baker, butcher etc. to deliver to your door and they usually whistled a tune as they came down the driveway. These days, I find it quite annoying if someone is whistling away randomly.

Depositphotos/filipw

I was recently in the supermarket and I could hear this phantom whistler near the fruit and veg section as I went in. You will know that you tend to keep meeting the same shoppers as you weave your way from one end of the building to the other, so I shot up to the alcoholic drinks section, the other end and worked my way back to the veg section, so I only had to put up with him whistling, 'The Hills are Alive with the Sound of Music', on the crisps and snacks aisle.

What a crazy world we live in. There's actually a World Whistling Championship in Louisburg, Carolina and David Morris from Dobcross, Lancashire won it once in 2003. Geert Chatrou from Holland is a three-time world champion and is a full-time professional whistler. *'I used to be a nurse, but just doing between 75 and 100 concerts a year earns me twice as much. I'm travelling with 'Cirque du Sol' and I open the show as a ringmaster. At one point I whistle, 'Twinkle, Twinkle, Little Star' and then go into a duet with a violinist backed by an orchestra.'*

Sniffing

I am talking here about a sudden drawing of air into the nose, not the use of snuff, Vick's vapours or banned substances. While I understand that allergies can create a desire to sniff, if you are trapped by someone sniffing incessantly for no apparent reason, it is not nice. I end up waiting for the next sudden 'intake of nasal air' and can pretty much work out when it will happen. I was on a train going from Norwich to London and the passenger opposite was sniffing every nine seconds. I estimated that would be 840 sniffs for the whole journey. Fortunately, he got off at Ipswich.

Wobbly Legs

I've experienced this infrequently in close proximity, but even that's too often and I'm not talking rickety chairs or table-legs. When I was training to be a teacher, I used to attend history lectures, where tables were set together in long rows and there was a guy, Dick 'Stack' Stevens who used to wobble his legs from side to side, giving slight continuous movement to the table he was on. He never seemed to notice that he always had a table to himself. I was on the tube recently and a guy was non-stop wobbling his legs for a couple of minutes, then stopped for 15 seconds, then off he'd go again. I just had to close my eyes and, fortunately, when I opened them later on the journey, he had gone.

Children

This is not a slight on children. It's the fact that children have now become baby goats. If you 'google' 'photos of kids', you'll find pictures of children, not young goats. Here's a real kid and another 'kid' who could soon be in a bit of trouble.

Plasters

Our world is one of ingenuity and inventiveness, so why can't we devise plasters that stay on the fingers, rather than coming loose as soon as they 'see' the 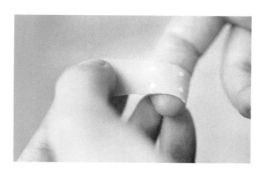 tap water? We must be going backwards.

As a young lad, a plaster (made of fabric) would be rolled around my cut finger. It stayed on (and on), slowly getting a darker tinge every day, despite hand washing, until it had to be physically removed, possibly days later. The adhesive was far superior than it is these days. I've purchased every variety on the chemists' shelves, with the inevitable result- failure. You wash your hands and it's not long before the unravelling process starts. I have found that, in an emergency, 'duct/gaffer' tape is the perfect solution, though the pain of removal, as it pulls out hair, is not to be recommended.

And a few more things....

- Why do people run a **hot bath,** then wait 15 to 20 minutes before getting in, by which time the water has cooled down and they add more hot water?

- Why do people wear **shorts in the middle of winter?** Why do really old men, in summer, wear **long socks, shorts, a tie and a jacket** together?

- You feel something very **large in your shoe.** It is so uncomfortable and it feels like a rock. You shake out the object and actually it's the size of a grain of sand.

- When England are playing football in the World Cup in some far away country, why do people insist on having **flags** flapping away on their cars, or draping them across the front of their houses?

- I don't have the best hearing I admit, so if I am talking to someone at a **call centre,** would they please make sure a) there isn't background noise from the other operatives competing for my attention, b) please ensure they have even a reasonable grasp of English, and c) that they understand how to relate to the customer. I recently spoke to someone who was representing a British company, but based abroad. He went to talk to someone to clarify something I needed to know. On his return, he said, "*So sorry to delay you sir. Are you having a nice cup of tea?*"

- How is it that you **ring a company** and when the call is connected, they say, 'Please select from the following eight options'? You choose and then they say,  'Select from these five options.' I've even known there to be another round! Anyway, I get confused and press any one and I tend to find whoever answers it, will put me through to a person to deal with it.

- Why do I forget to remove **tissues from my pockets**, before I put the trousers in the washing machine? They morph into thousands of wispy bits that are a nightmare to brush away from all the items that have been contaminated.

- Why is it always **hot in the UK** when I go abroad on holiday?

- **I go into a shop** and pay with a £10 note. The cashier gives me the receipt, with a £5 note on the top of that AND THEN the coins on top of that. You have to be pretty nifty to avoid dropping the lot. I know what you are saying: just use a credit card.

- I am not a fan of **chewing gum**, especially if I get it stuck to my trousers, when some idiot has attached it to the underside of the table I am sitting at. They estimate Oxford Street in London has 300,000 pieces stuck on the pavements and it costs you and me, via council tax, £1.50 per square metre to clean it off (so says 'Keep Britain Tidy).

- How come by appearing on a reality TV show, you become a **celebrity?**

- I pick up the **roll of Sellotape**, ready to wrap a parcel. Why can I never find the end?

- Why do people park in '**disabled parking bays**' when they do not have a 'blue badge'?

- What is the point of **car alarms?** They go off willy-nilly and no one takes any notice: we assume it's gone off by mistake.

- Why do some people who **vape** blow clouds of horrible strawberry flavoured smoke into the air and up my nostrils? I thought pure cigarette smoke was disgusting.

Unsplash/Itay Kabola

- We have always found it difficult to have conversations about **death and dying,** and to me that includes using those terms, harsh as they may seem. To me that's the reality of the situation, rather than to say someone has 'passed'. I know how upsetting it is if a family pet dies (sorry 'passes') but I am a little surprised that this is now the term also used for a dog or cat's departure from this life. I always associated "passed" with a good exam outcome.

- **Mountains of flowers** appear at or close to the spot of where someone has died tragically, maybe in a car crash. The sad bit is seeing flowers wither and decay in the following days. I always remember being confused when flowers were 'pelted' at Princess Diana's hearse. I though people threw things in disgust, not in grief

- What is going in our gardens? People are claiming that they are **'rewilding'**; encouraging nature. Come on, it's just an excuse for laziness. In my manicured backyard, there are pots of Begonias, Busy Lizzies, Fuchsias  etc. The bees and other insects love my garden (the snails and slugs: too much so).

- Why do people **walk in the woods**, where they are surrounded by the beautiful sights and sounds of nature and yet walk around with ear pieces, or those giant headphones?

- How sad it is to see a **baby being pushed in a buggy,** without eye-to-eye contact, as the parent is too busy flicking through their mobile phone. I've even experienced the child talking to the parent who is oblivious, as they look at their social media posts.

- I've had enough of people being interviewed – especially politicians – who use the **word 'look'**. It's not very easy for me to 'look' when they are on the radio. Anyway, what do they want me to look at? The other one is when they say **'listen'** to the interviewer.

- I'm asked to tick a box indicating which **age group** I am in. I look down and there is maybe 16-21, 22-30 etc and then suddenly it jumps to 65+. I feel I've been written off altogether.

- **Union bosses miss a trick.** It's hard enough for them to keep the public on their side when there's a dispute going on. Instead of just talking about 'our members', they should emphasise that this is to benefit the public as well, for example for safety reasons, or to avoid shortages of staff e.g. in the NHS.

- It's September, so **Halloween is coming** (in 8½ weeks time)! Hot on its heels will be shops filled with **Christmas**. Then, joy of joys, on the first day of November (if not before), 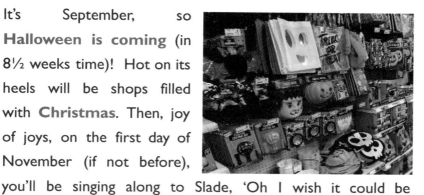 you'll be singing along to Slade, 'Oh I wish it could be Christmas everyday.' Lovely.

- People making **announcements you can't hear** or understand are extremely irritating. Tube train drivers have to be the worst. 'Mine clos du.' This I believe translates to, 'Mind the closing doors.'

- Why do people pay £25 or more to go to a rock concert and then spend half the evening **talking away to someone else**, while you are trying to listen to your favourite band. Oh, and you spend ages finding a strategic spot with a half decent view and the **tallest person in the hall walks** in and stands right in front of you, so you end up looking at the middle of their back, rather than the stage.

- Chew **gum** if you wish, but please do it with your mouth closed, rather than showing your teeth and gums.

- Are you like me, in that trying to get the **handwash pump** to open up and work properly is one of the challenges of our time?

- Why are people so **obsessed with their phones?** A third of young people aged 18-30 accept that they have an addiction and it is said that addicts touch their phones around 5,400 times a  day and half of users check their phone between midnight and 5am. Travel on the tube and you will see most people on their phones, either texting, playing a game or watching a film.

- **Signage:** you are told not to park in front of a dilapidated prefab garage as it is in use 24 hours a day, or the driveway is in 'constant use'. I would agree your local high street might well be in constant use. Why don't they just put, 'No parking: access required'?

- **Bins in hotel rooms:** you get those tiny pedal bins, but when you stand on the handle to open the bin, the bin shoots forward.

- Why do sports people say they gave 110%? What's wrong with 100%?

VIII. FASHION

Clothing

Why is it that a **design of clothing** - shape, colour etc., is *'in'* this year, with everyone going 'Ooh, ah, that is amazing,' then next year people guffaw when they see someone wearing last year's item? Don't bin it, because it will come back "in" eventually.

The **button fly** should not be allowed within a million miles of a pair of trousers. Don't ever be in a hurry to go to the toilet with the button fly, or you could be in for an unhappy accident. Once you've managed to undo them, you now have another five minutes spent to button them up and then another two when one pops out (the button I mean). I am told, not from personal experience of course, well not for 40 years anyway, that tearing off trousers in a moment of passion requires the good old zip for the best/quickest results.

I wish all **shirts were 'non-iron'**. I have several that I can screw up, jump on and still they can be worn without the need to be ironed. The trouble is I can never be sure when I'm shopping if it will turn out as a 'non-iron'.

I get it home and realise it's another 'creaser'. Maybe I should take the item in the shop's dressing rooms and screw it up and judge the outcome before I buy.

Sweatshirts with the fashion companies' logos: what's all that about? They have got you over a barrel. You are paying THEM to advertise their brand!

Obscene language is something I do NOT like to see on clothing, even if I occasionally utter such words, when I drop something on my foot (only then of course). I was in a store and there was this guy with a child in the trolley: the picture says it all.

Kauan Vargasn

My personal 'favourite' not to like…..
torn/ripped jeans. My advice is go and get a pair of standard jeans (cheaper). Open the kitchen drawer and at no cost to yourself, utilise

scissors, knives etc, to create a unique style to impress all your friends

'**Jogging Bottoms**' are a fashion 'must' for some people. For me, do they look good worn in public? I think not: perfect for around the house or at the gym.

Let's hear it for '**harem pants**'. I couldn't dream up a more bizarre fashion item, but hang on, you can buy a pair from multiple on-line sites if you are so inclined. They are described as, 'The perfect gift for anyone who wants to be comfy and stylish.' Great to satisfy the hippy in you maybe. I guess they could be useful when you go shopping. You wouldn't need a carrier bag; just stuff your groceries down your pants, so to speak.

When ever was the **poncho** a fashionable item for men or women? It keeps raising its head above the parapet and gets the thumbs down. It may look good in its natural setting in South America, but in the UK no. If you really, really want one, buy a square of cloth, lay it on the floor, draw round a dinner plate with a black felt tip, cut out the circle with scissors and, 'hey presto'.

Bodies

Now I know 'goths' love their black imagery and the desire for lipstick to match their attire. Ok, no problem, but as a general rule to women (or men) out there, my advice is do NOT wear **black lipstick**. Also do not be tempted to pay for **'lip augmentation'**. Those sausage lips are not a good look, but neither is **'breast augmentation'**.

For me the other strange one is the desire for some women to **bronze their skin** (in the style of Katie Price?). One product advertises as follows: *"Bronzer is a multitasking makeup product that truly does it all....to define our features as pure 'wow'."* No it doesn't.

'Anything Goes' probably best sums up the way of the world fashion-wise these days, and hey why not? Go for it!

67

Tattoos

This gets its own special heading, as it's the symbol of the 'modern age', gaining growing acceptance in the 1990s onwards, although it was always a tradition amongst soldiers and sailors with the obligatory anchor and maybe 'love' and 'hate', imprinted on each set of knuckles. It was generally seen as something for the working classes and in Roman times they were used to identify those considered unworthy!

Let's get straight to it: I am not a fan of tattoos. If you have observed an elderly person who has carried one for years, what was a plum is now definitely a wrinkled prune and any writing is a series of faded squiggles. They've also possibly lived for 50 years carrying the name of the woman/man they once loved, but stopped doing

Unsplash/Natherlie-stimpfl

so 27 years earlier. Be careful what you wish for! Pins and studs are to be recommended, as they can be removed and the wearer is back to 'as was' condition within months.

My suggestion: no tattoos until you reach 65, then go mad if you wish: they'll look pristine for the rest of your life. It could be expensive though, as there will be more of you to cover.

While I don't look the other way when I see tattoos, I am kind of fascinated to understand what makes people completely cover their heads and bodies and, I'm being sexist here, why would any woman want to cover their legs with them? What I loved in my 20s, is not necessarily what I appreciate now. Imagine, that tattoo that is 'cool' now, may cause distress every time you look in the mirror in just 20 years' time

Builders' Bum

I guess it's not exactly a fashion statement, but it's certainly a statement.

It seems statutory for those doing physical work, to bend over and show us their 'all'.

IX. CULTURE & RELIGION

Multiculturalism

We live in a **multicultural society** and there's no clearer sign than that in London, where I live now. The many nationalities and cultures living amicably side by side, has brought a richness, vibrancy and diversity which it is a pleasure to be part of. There are pockets of people who do not engage, but they are the great minority and most want to experience and be part of 'Britishness', whatever that concept actually is!

One thing we do stand for is openness, so I am not comfortable with wearers of the niqab (only the eyes visible). You see a wife walking on a hot summer's day, face (and body) fully covered and alongside is the husband in jeans and T-shirt. Showing your face is crucial to human interaction, to assess what people are thinking and a woman covered as described, will struggle to find any kind of paid work, especially something like teaching or social work.

I recall as a teacher doing drama work with children wearing **masks**. How illuminating that was. Even when the children knew who the wearer was, they showed concern on their faces and some showed real anxiety. In the discussion that followed, these

70

9-year-olds explained they looked at the face to judge what the person was thinking or feeling- especially their teacher! Without knowing, they felt anxious, even worried. Even at a young age, they are already using visual cues to make judgements.

I would add that I am a fan of the **hijab**, an item of attire which frames a woman's face perfectly.

Pexels/PNW productions

Sexual Orientation

I am very comfortable living in an age where people are free to express their sexuality. It is an affront to human values to know there are still 64 countries which criminalise homosexuality (mainly in Africa) and in 11 the death penalty applies. However, I do find the debate on terms such as 'gender neutral' a challenge to comprehend.

Singer Sam Smith states, 'I feel just as much a woman as I am a man.' The website 'teentalk.ca' lists some of the different genders that are out there and apart from those most of us are familiar with, there is 'non-binary, agender, pangender, genderqueer, two-spirit, third gender', and all, none or a combination of these. The site 'sexualdiversity.org' goes further and lists 105 distinctive genders. I am lucky that I won't be around to sort all of that out!

X. ANTI-SOCIAL BEHAVIOUR

You probably think this has already been dealt with (bicycles on pavements etc). Far from it...

Litter

Why do some people think it's someone else's job to pick up the litter they have dropped? Walk along any street and there it is- plastic food containers, bottles, cigarette ends and the

Pexels/Ugur Tandogan

rest. Travel along stretches of motorway – the first view people coming from abroad may have of the UK as they roll off the ferry – and rubbish of all kinds is there to be seen.

I remember watching a man open his car door and proceed to drop his rubbish on the floor - mainly from McDonalds. Why didn't I approach him? He was bigger than me.

Fly Tipping

I feel for those farmers who find their lanes blocked with rubbish just dumped out of the back of a truck. Prison should be a real possibility for those caught. At the very least,

if caught, the 'tipper' should have to pick it up, put it on a truck and then dump it in their own front garden and then, within seven days after everyone now knows the perpetrator, s/he has to reload it on a truck and take it to the tip.

Hedges

I'm talking here about the many people who, bit by bit, allow their front hedge to creep over the pavement, as if they are laying claim to the street as part of their property. Make sure you are not walking in pairs, pushing a buggy, nor yet riding on a mobility scooter.

Sunbeds

Who are those numpties who get up at the crack of dawn, just to claim a sunbed, so that by the time I'm down, they've all been claimed? Why won't holiday hotels enforce the 'rule' displayed nearby:, *'All towels will be removed from vacant sunbeds?'* I've only witnessed it once, so that at that hotel, in the morning there were no towels out. The photo you can see was taken at 5.30 am by the side of one hotel pool. Go on YouTube and put in 'Sun Bed Wars' and you'll see what I mean

Graffiti

Now there's good graffiti and there's bad graffiti. With the latter I suspect an inferiority complex and low self-esteem leads someone to feel a need to be noticed. These examples blight our

cities and towns. It's hard to feel sorry for those who died in the act of this vandalism, falling from bridges, being electrocuted, or hit by trains.

Now we come to the opposite of those cretins; the amazing skill employed by 'amateur' artists producing works of art that are frankly breath-taking.

Pixabay/Tomasz Hanarz

Why do people paint their house numbers on dustbins? To avoid looking for a brush and paint, why not go to your local DIY shop and buy the numbers at very little cost? You can get three sticker numbers for 99p on ebay, postage free!

Irresponsible Dog Owners

If you'd asked me ten years ago what I thought about dogs, I'd have said, 'Not a lot.' I'd have expanded on that saying it was because they bark and defecate and you can guarantee I'll step in it and take it into my house. Some breeds really smell too.

My stance has softened somewhat by my experience of my daughter and son- in- law's dog, namely a greyhound, that rarely barks and does not smell and now my son and daughter in law have a cockapoo, so that's a double whammy of positivity.

The fact remains though that some dog walkers are indifferent to the 'package' their dog leaves on the grass or pavement. As bad as that, are the dog walkers who bag up the excrement and then either drop the plastic bag on the ground, or hang it up in a tree. While some may be coming back after the walk to collect the hanging object, my experience is that the bag will be there until someone else deals with it. 28% of dog owners admitted confidentially in a survey that they don't pick up their dog's 'mess' (Credit: The Guardian).

I was in Norwich city centre and witnessed the behaviour of someone I can only describe as 'low life'. He had two large, aggressive looking breeds of dog. One squatted outside Marks & Spencer. The man stopped and allowed the dog to leave an enormous pile of excrement on the pavement. I plucked up the courage to approach him and queried, 'Would you like that on your clothes and shoes?' He said (in his broad Norwich accent), '*I hent got a bag hev I?*' I pointed out that he could use the Haribo sweet bag that he had dropped on the floor previously. He just walked off, went round the corner and allowed the other dog to do exactly the same: big dogs, big poos.

XI. GAMBLING

Everyone has the right to pursue activities that bring them pleasure and while I don't 'get it', I am aware that people enjoy playing a 'fruit machine' or the odd bet or 'flutter' on the horses or the National Lottery. It is enjoyed by millions; most responsibly.

My concern is the negative, indeed devastating outcomes for many who become addicted. This leads to bankruptcy; family break up and homelessness in some cases. Why do

Pexels/Pavel Danilyuk

governments not act to reign in this menace? They are, it seems, at the behest of the gambling companies, who are very powerful lobbyists, so progress in curbing gambling addiction is slow. One MP accepted hospitality and tickets from betting firms for almost £8000 in 2021.

Football is but one example, where you will see ex footballers such as Peter Crouch, promoting the company Paddy Power and Jeff Stelling extolling the benefits of using Sky Bet.

Nine Premier League teams are linked directly to betting firms. To Norwich City's credit, they changed tack when their supporters expressed outrage in 2021 just as they were close to agreeing a deal with Asian betting firm BK8. They pulled out just in time and signed a deal with Lotus cars instead.

This comment appeared on a social media platform attributed to someone called Steve:

'Gambling has basically taken away my whole life. It has taken away my integrity, my mind, my soul, my spirit, my energy, my everything. In a lot of people's minds, I seem successful, as I have a car and am educated, but deep down inside I am dying.'

XII. LAW & ORDER

Scammers are undoubtedly evil, especially the way they prey on the vulnerable. I regularly get such calls. Often the phone just rings and if you don't pick up it stops. That is very annoying when I am having my afternoon nap. Scammers have pretended that there is a problem with my internet and that they can sort it. What a load of tosh.

One strategy is to 'turn' the conversation. Ask them if they are having a nice day, what they are wearing, or something even more personal. They'll soon ring off. You'd have many more tales to tell, I am sure. I have had a sister in law and three friends 'scammed', so it can happen to anyone.

Crime has increased over the last few years and for certain it is due to the **reduction in police numbers**. Again and again I hear the mantra, '20,000 new police officers on our streets.' Am I being a wee bit cynical in thinking they are replacing the 21,000 police officers who are leaving through stress, pay and working conditions and U turns by their political masters?

We used to have lots of Police Community Support Officers. While they have limited powers of arrest, they are a deterrent for sure, walking around the streets. In Norfolk, they were all made redundant in 2018 and in London's Metropolitan police, their numbers have fallen by 32% since 2015.

In my own quiet street, there has been at least one car stolen. My neighbour was woken at night by a noise on the street outside his house. He looked out, saw his car being jacked up, with the **catalytic converter being cut away and stolen**. I can say with confidence that if the thieves' van was stopped in the middle of the night, with many catalytic converters in the back, unless they can be traced to a specific vehicle, the police have no grounds for an arrest or successful prosecution. One person on my street went outside in the early morning, to see someone on a bicycle going off with **items from her car boot**. He even had the temerity to say 'sorry' as he cycled off.

Apart from the horrendously low detection rate, sometimes I feel the **deterrents are not sufficient to stop people** committing crime, because they will walk free from the courts. There was a social media post on 'TikTok' telling people that stores in the West End of London were to be looted. This led to police clashing with (mainly) youths and they made nine arrests (no doubt accusing the police of brutality). I can guarantee they were treated leniently by the courts: after all our prisons are full. There has been an epidemic of gangs entering small shops like Tesco Locals and walking out with goods, with the security guard unable to stop them.

Two sisters walked out of a supermarket in Norwich, wheeling a trolley piled high with items worth more than £1,800. They returned to the same supermarket, but were caught as they attempted to wheel off another trolley-full, worth £610. The defence solicitor said they were struggling financially due to the cost-of-living crisis. In fact, despite the value of goods stolen, they only had to repay costs of £62 and a fine of £80 each

My own solution to 'low level' crime? **Bring back the stocks!** In times gone by, every village and town would have wooden stocks and the perpetrators of  crime were put in there so the community could 'right the wrong' by pelting the individual with rotten food. I bet they never offended again. Interestingly the law allowing the use of the stocks still exists! Seriously though, I think there should be more 'payback' schemes whereby an offender in a hi-vis jacket should be employed in public view on the streets, putting right their wrongs e.g., litter picking, cleaning graffiti or doing painting jobs.

XIII. AND FINALLY

Just to show you that I do not grind my teeth or throw my hands up in despair at our world. There is so much that is positive and these are just a few of such things:

- **The internet.** I would never have written this book without the help of a computer. I use the computer for emails, for research and to follow my love of music.

- **Inventions** of every kind that have changed our lives. Let me pick some that are easily overlooked: Velcro (no need to learn to tie your laces any more), paper clips, safety pins, springs, the zip, post it notes, duct tape, tea bags, toilet paper, button holes, can openers and many, many more of course. Where would we be without them?

- The **'Freedom Pass'** is so liberating. In London it means that, because I am over 60 (by some distance unfortunately), I can travel around the capital and beyond at no cost by TfL train, bus or on the tube after 9am. Those of a certain age say that this freedom to travel around has made a big impact on their well-being.

- People who do **good deeds.** I have the perfect example. Prior to my hip operations, I needed crutches for assistance. As I was struggling along in the rain one day, with a shopping bag somehow attached to one crutch, a young lady stopped me and asked if she could help by carrying my shopping bag or, better still, drive me home. I was very touched. In other situations, if someone falls in the street, there's always someone who goes over and offers help. I try to do an act of kindness every day, even if it's just opening a door for someone.

- **Generosity.** It was only after George Michael's death that his acts of kindness and generosity came to light. He gave millions to charities like 'Childline'. Bill Gates has given much of his fortune away and there is an organisation called the 'Patriotic Millionaires' in the UK (and US), who canvas for the rich to be taxed more highly for the benefit of the nation.

- The **ethnic mix** of a place like London, where I have the opportunity to have a life enriched by meeting lovely people and learning more about cultures and practices that I knew little of and getting to enjoy foods that stimulate the taste buds.

- Despite my (well founded?) comments about the political scene in the UK, we remain a **democracy**. My conversations with a taxi driver who still has relatives in Afghanistan, was a stark reminder of what things could be like in so many parts of the world. He was effusive in his praise of Britain, a country where he is free to practise his beliefs, without fear or favour and has embraced British culture and values completely and is a hard-working tax payer. The same would apply, without doubt to the great majority of people who seek asylum here, running from persecution and worse, elsewhere in the world.

- Those who choose to **do a job for its worth**, not for the financial rewards.

- People who **face up to challenges.** Lloyd Scott ran the London Marathon in a 1940s diving suit- rubberised canvas, copper helmet and lead lined boots. He crossed the line five days, eight hours, 29 minutes and 46 seconds later. *'When I was diagnosed with cancer, I needed to know it was not the end. I have come through it and wanted to inspire anyone else diagnosed not to give up hope.'* Jane Tomlinson, who was terminally ill, is the only person who has run a marathon while having chemotherapy. She raised £1.75million before her death. George Mallory was asked in 1923 why he had wanted to climb Everest and he replied, *'Because it's there.'* These are the real heroes- and many more besides, not overpaid footballers, or the Z list reality 'stars'.

- I admire people who have **passions,** whether in their work or their hobbies**.** The standout character has to be everyone's hero- David Attenborough, who I first saw on black and white TV on Zoo Quest in 1958.

- I love the **positive, 'can-do' attitude** of many young people, despite the fact that some of their peers let them down badly.

- People who **make me laugh** are important to me, as well as having the ability to laugh at themselves. It's great when you find something so funny, you even laugh when you are on your own. The TV programme 'Fawlty Towers' is one of those for sure.

- **Quality service** in restaurants and shops.

- I love being around **positive people**. Negativity is awful to be around. In every workplace there are the 'radiators'; the people that have that warmth and positivity, and then the 'drains' who can suck the lifeblood out of the workplace. Remember two phrases: first, *'Don't go through life, grow through life'* and, *'If you do what you've always done, you'll always get what you've always got'*. Make the change that's within you!

I could go on and on, but I'm not going to, I'm just off to eat some chocolate (apparently, it's good for you).

Printed in Great Britain
by Amazon

33717137R00050